POETRY MINE

POETRY MINE

The Dayshift

Geoff Jones

Caneri Press

First published in 2009 by:
Caneri Press

ISBN 978-0-9561921-0-3

Printed and bound in Great Britain by:
Proprint Remus House, Coltsfoot Drive, Woodston
Peterborough PE2 9JX

Foreword

I recall the poem, 'The Hunchback in the Park' by Dylan Thomas as a subject for discussion among the group where I first met Geoff Jones, on the Open Studies poetry writing course at the University of Warwickshire. Little did I realise I had unwittingly played straight into his hands, as the discussion extended into the university bar and we became embroiled in the arts of reminiscence, poetry-and Wales.

Geoff went on to study for an MA and returned to succeed me as a creative writing tutor at Warwick. In recent years he has gone through good and bad times, but always the urge to write has winked and nudged, ebbed and flowed, until the only outcome had to be the book you have before you.

Geoff's poems capture the essences of time and place; the landscape of Nantyglo and the slopes of the Milfraen; adolescent posturing in Brynmawr Square's Italian café with Elvis on the jukebox; the ever-present darkness of the pit-the underground world of Willie-John Davies and those anonymous 'men in Dai Caps'.

Therefore, it really does 'give me great pleasure', as I am bound to say at this point, to endorse this book; to wish it and its author well; but most of all, to invite you to join Geoff on his journey: 'up the overgrown path/in search of our way-marked stile,' as he writes in 'To Earth'; there to rest and enjoy the view.

John Alcock
Former Director of Open Studies Creative Writing, University of Warwick
Associate of the Welsh Academi

Acknowledgements

Acknowledgements are due to the editors of the following publications in which some of these poems first appeared: *Aesthetica, Broadside X, Cannon's Mouth, Chillout, Earth Works, Lookout, Raw Edge, Tamworth Writing, The Journal, The Magazine and Word Play.*

Special thanks to all members of Cannon Poets for their help and advice and a big debt of gratitude to John Alcock who inspired me to write seriously at the University of Warwick. His advice and guidance in the preparation of this collection has been invaluable.

Alongside John, a very big thank you to Bill Parkinson for his constant faith and encouragement.

Other people too, have had an influence through workshops, public readings and various courses including Phil Emery, Sybil Ruth, David Hart, Julie Boden and Roz Goddard.

In addition, David Fine whose website www.lit-net.org led me to an award by the Literary Consultancy of London which produced a helpful critique on several of the poems included in the following pages.

I am grateful to Nigel Thomas who, in addition to translating the first poem – *Nantyglo* – inspired me to speak Welsh and to continue learning the language.

And thanks to fellow school rugby player Ian Wilson, whose compliments concerning *Where the Boots Take You* (no pun intended!) helped the final push into print.

Finally, a very sincere thank you to Fran who has performed many roles including that of a sounding board, editor and meticulous proof reader.

For

Mam and Dad

who gave everything

The past is a foreign country:
they do things differently there.

L P Hartley (1895-1972)
The Go-Between

Contents

Blackthorn

In spite of the wind
almost bending them horizontal

the branches
of the tall trees

flailing the glass panes
in frustration

gripped their blossoms
determined to hang

on to the symbols
of coming spring

not for them
autumn's wrenching

or the lingering
demise of winter

just the comfort
of a summer promise

to see them through
this April rage

Nantyglo*

High up at the head of the valley
where the stream's face hardened

under the breath of December
and where the mountain guardians

received their delivery of white cloaks
fashioned by swirling winds

and moonlight flooded
the land

the mining village nestled
in new disguise

frost nibbling away at its feet

Nantyglo: stream of coal

Nantyglo (Cymraeg)

Uchel i fyny ar flaen y cwm
lle caledai wyneb y nant

dan anadl mis Rhagfyr
a lle câi ceidwaid y mynydd

eu rhodd o fentyll gwynion
wedi'u llunio gan wyntoedd troelli

a llifai'r lloergan
y wlad

nythai'r pentref glofaol
dan rith newydd

cnoai llorrew ar ei draed

Translation by Nigel Thomas

Dying Language

Just a few Welsh names lived on in Nantyglo
all others buried in the bottom of the long graveyard
behind my Baptist chapel

headstones carved out in Welsh and as the people
died over the years
English infiltrated the struggle
for life up the cemetery hill

removing words
without protest from the dead
for by then it was well into its death throes

slaughtered by epitaphs
deeply engraved in English
but next to the name burials lay *Ffoesmaen Road*

surviving the cull
tracking a way
to *The Ffoesmaen Inn*

where once a Baptist minister
on horseback
having galloped up
from the Vale of Usk in the mid 19th Century

proclaimed his sermons
in Cymraeg
his success raising
Hermon above the rooftops

a chapel of faith in the language of Cymru

Resigned

Resigned in look
around motorway restaurant

you drift slowly
clearing tables of unwanted food

people's leftovers muck debris

just like you
unwanted by the steelworks

worked out
no mates to share snap time

you breathe the smoke-free air
mentally polluted

Mam

She sat where she always sat
pinafored

pale

small in the high backed chair
cornered by table and fireplace

silent

nerves twanging away
like Welsh longbows at Crécy

arrows parried by the work ethic

until that too
gave way

leaving her
grasping for reality

Connections

You are the woman lying
in the dappled shadows

of the weeping willow
at the edge

of the long garden
in which

in one corner
a large towel

hanging from
a rotary line

swings slowly
in the afternoon breeze

which gently shakes
the fingertips

of the flowering cherry
bypassed by a cabbage white

on another mazy quest
to the purple buddleia

lazily leaning out
from the tall shrub

behind which
cluck the hens

who laid those
delicious eggs

you served this morning
for breakfast

Remembering

Thirty six years
since you left
but the tears always well

seeing you so young and happy
never to age as I
and the girls now fully grown

I cannot hear your voice
nor footstep on the stair
nor feel your head rest gently on my chest

I reach out to stroke your face
to run my hands down your soft cheeks
to cup your dimpled chin

but you are beyond touch
as I am with the past
that comes and visits

carrying the memories
of what was
and what might have been

Hafod-y-ddôl

Dumbfounded I stand and stare at the emptiness
front gates long gone just two stone posts remain

the stable ghost is no more for there are no stables
razed are the grey walls and weeds choke the yard

a soldier line of trees buckle in the wind of autumn
unclothed arms shivering after the lost summer

I hear the echoes of a silent bell
arresting ghostly voices and playground energies

our houses gold Gwillym Gwent
purple Penllywn and the white of Lancaster – all surrendered

I remember the might of your dragon red navy blue and yellow
but the authority quicksand has sucked you under
never to resurface

I see you no more old friend but even now hear you teaching
'Aequam Servare Mentem'*

*School Motto: To preserve a calm mind'

Underground

Down in the depths of a steep-staired basement
where Willie-John Davies is brewing strong tea
darkness is holed by suspended lighting
flooding over tables so players can see

Upstairs in the institute reading room
sit tired old miners turning news pages
ex-butties of Willie-John sprightly as ever
stands up to new levels deserving his wages

Abandoned on slag heaps of dust lunged lives
blue scarred faces stare enviously below
at cloth capped Willie-John dry mouthed miner
continuously chewing creating saliva flow

No more pick axing in low roofed tunnels
or deep water working shovelling coal
no more dread of gas explosions
for Willie-John Davies has a positive goal

Booking out snooker tables taking money
Willie-John Davies short stocky and stern
ensuring silence aids concentration
with raw teenagers quick to learn

Silence in contrast to the clanging of shovels
the light not black though still very dim
but Willie-John Davies can lift up his bright eyes
and rest content the roof will never fall in

The Cut

(i) Tipton Cut

Can you pick those overhanging blackberries
and taste the essence of a rambling town

hear the narrow boat emerging from Doe Bank Bridge
its engine bursting into new life

see black clouds rising from the smoke stack
their smell of sulphur

reminding me of winter fires in Wales?

(ii) Bridge On The Cut

Unique Doe Bank Bridge
guards the dark narrow waters
always there for us

(iii) The Pin

The pin
on the rudder

tells me somebody's home
but I won't find out until they

show up

Frozen Time

Beating wings in protest
a swan slithers on splintered glass
frustrated by the frosted floor

ungloved hands of a willow
hang down in apparent sorrow
afraid to touch the frozen waterway

in its iced grip a long boat,
narrow red green redundant
lies tethered to needless moorings

but down the straight white highway
old coal barge ghosts drawn by horses
glide silently and disappear

The Broads
(National Railway Poster by Spender Pryse circa 1925)

I wondered if she came by LNER
the young woman in the
woollen bathing suit

white towelling robe
hanging from limp wrists
as if a Roman consul

standing in the bowels
of the becalmed boat
exhibiting herself haughtily

and at the stern
under a yellow striped canopy
hugging his knees with bowed head

a disconsolate bather
banished and dismissed
for the temptress has captivated

two more admirers in vested costumes
half out of the shallow broad
leaning casually on gunwale

smiling and staring
at the elevated spirit
gazing disdainfully down

in the middle ground a backstroker
windmills the water unaware
of the portrait before him

and behind him a triangular
brown sail bending with wind
glides behind reeds

its crew detached
from the siren
and departed train

Broadland

The last day of summer
drains palely away

joining the distant windmill
rendered surplus

once its own drainage days
had dried up

Still clutched
by a relentless landscape

its sail-less body
stands forlorn and becalmed

Two brown and disembodied sails
slide silently before me

catch a grateful wind
and move slowly out of my life

leaving me again
with the redundant tower

Looking Through Trees

As we drove north
I saw through the black trees

bare arms shivering in winter's chill
trunks charcoaled by fire

I saw through their sadness
the background of a new month

breaking into a gun-metalled year
like the sky looking down the barrel

of a quiet Nottingham afternoon
car swiftly and silently

speeding down dark avenues
eventually breaking through

the defences of the city to plunder
IKEA
a tundra of wood stretching endlessly across Northern Europe

Perito Moreno Glacier

Vast glacier
wall rising into peaks of white
like the adjacent Andes
fronts
the renewing ice field

stillness
suddenly shattered
like gunshot
as a slice of blue wall
slides into the lake
below
sending fountains
of water
high into the frozen air
splintering
into ice boats
floating away

forgotten

I swivel again
squinting through
sun's eyesight
waiting for the next
explosion

(*Coro Nacional de Gales/'Welsh National Choir' to Patagonia
May 2007*)

Tied Up

Like a pendulum swung into life
anchored boats right angled to shore

vigorously rock both ways
dancing to the rhythm

grateful fishing vessels create
surging into harbour

wired halyards smack
against metal masts

singing high pitched tunes
before the melodies

ease to their end

heading out to open sea
a solitary boat passes by

on the other side
ignoring the moored strangers

their Español flags
now drooping at half-mast

Rising Above

Rising above
a city in a gondola
is something
you don't do every day
but as we sailed
around
for the first time
viewing the glass
and concrete shoreline below
my stomach leapt
into my mouth
then slowly
sank
in harmony
with the downward sweep
of
The Eye

Tunnel
(Calke Abbey, Derby)

Giving more headroom than prisoners of war

the cut and cover tunnel –
carrying a brick barrelled ceiling

some sixty metres long from garden to estate boundary
through which gardeners stooped and peered on their way

to and from working for the gentry
promenading their pleasure gardens

exhibiting finery
like the preening of their peacocks –

must have fulfilled the same purpose
for the workers

sick and tired
of seeing such inescapable riches

and always being kept in the dark

knew their place
was not for them

Heat

She nudges me awake
and like a new lover

knows she will embrace me all day

a distant scooter like a bee
hums briefly then ceases

a whispered command
the barking dog

retreats into silence
a door closes softly

she caresses me
once more

To Earth

Even in death he was adept at hiding
for we were not aware of him

on our way up the overgrown path
in search of our way-marked stile

it was only when we retraced our steps
we noticed him lying there in red

as if stunned in mid flight
neck strained forward

exposed sharp teeth
and bushy brush splayed behind

demonstrating his old turn of speed

Hedgehog

Early September afternoon
in the pale sunshine

he came in from the field
squeezing under the gate

and crept slowly towards
the bowl of water where

he leaned for many minutes
drinking in his reward

leaving the way he had come
disappearing in the tall grass

mid October he returned
out of hibernation we thought

to enjoy autumn sunshine
in our newly dug flower bed

we were wrong for the flies
like vultures buzzing around

his open eyes told us he was going
and later we laid him to rest

under the shade of the weeping birches

Men In Dai Caps

Men in Dai Caps stumble
into chill dawns

the clump of hobnailed boots
echoing through tier-terraced streets

throated woollen mufflers clinging
to determined jaws

jagged blue lines etching foreheads
facing the hungry earth that eats

swallows digests and vomits them
out in a gush of blackness

matched by the black river
flowing through

the detritus
of the monster mine

Y Fenni*

Overlooking the old town
seven hills discernible unlike those of Rome
guard The Gateway to Wales

Pen-y-Fal or the Sugar Loaf
silent and still belying her volcanic outline
snow bringing her name to life in winter

broad shouldered Blorenge
gripping the Newport-Brecon canal
like a narrow belt around its waist

the brothers Skirrid Fawr and Fach
lying down in slumber
Gulliver-like figures tramping along their backs

while the old town once occupied by friendly G.I.'s
gives way to the tourist invaders
who plunder her weekly markets

Y Fenni: Abergavenny

Reclaiming The Language

In the mountains and valleys our names are returning
to their roots
Huw and Dafydd Mair and Sioned
reclaiming identities ruthlessly stifled by an alien language

our own language dug up and cast aside on rubbish tips
of profit
so we were left with scraps of words quickly
devoured before starvation led us to a forced diet
of foreign words

But now the signs are there . . .
Abergavenny
Y Fenni
Crickhowell
Crug Hywel
Ebbw Vale
Glyn Ebwy

. . . road sign translations still giving way
but at least we are signalling our intentions
our intentions to reclaim our Welsh from classroom corners

where offenders were sent in disgrace
forced to wear wooden Welsh knots
for being themselves

Dedicated to Nigel Thomas

Mining The Past

Squatting on haunches under flat caps
semi-strangled by silk mufflers

encased in watch-chained waistcoats
institute walls for chair backs

dark eyes squinting against the light
in between drags on fags and pipe pulls

they poured out their prophecies
to anyone who might listen

philosophers intellectuals scholars
the Platos and Aristotles of coal mining

we had no time to stop and listen
for we had joined other factions

we were jiving to the new Rock 'n' Roll
considered their talk outmoded

for youth knew better
disregarded the wizened old men

thought they cut sad figures
but when I returned

to share my own philosophy
they were no longer there

even the benches that replaced
their singular territories

were empty

Beware Great Woolly Whites!
(visitwales.co.uk poster)

With water streaming
whale like down his lycra

he teeters on crests as the surging surf
rushes him to shore

on the beach
it stands statuesque

staring at the incomer
ears pricked as do all its breed

wandering the sandy pastures
wrapped up in woollen coats

still walking on waves
the invader must puzzle

at the strange way to keep
a warm Welsh welcome

from a woolly white
staring

at the surfer racking up
a perfect cut back

and it may hurt a little
at the great white's indifference

but in 38 years
farmer Henry Hughes

cannot recall
a single sheep attack

Milfraen

Entering the head of the valley
I drove down its spine
mountains like ribs
rising on its flanks

Mynydd-carn-y-cefn facing my exhausted village
steep sides blanketed in bracken
too far away to be a real friend

unlike The Milfraen
our very own mountain
gentle slopes leaning away to a glaciated roof

sustaining sheep on her upper slopes
an encircling dry stoned wall failing
to curb the woollen raiders from nosing over
our dustbins at night

never to be seen at dawn
drawn back to the familiar pastures
of our guardian

still keeping watch over
our village which sat in the stern
of the U-boat running all the way to the sea.

The Pits

Beneath our house
pits honeycombed the valley

beneath our street
miners travelled their own roadways

when I left
the winding wheels were winding down

and miners travelled on the surface
in their own cars no longer those of their masters

Above the English pit
where I now live

the canal tramways have disappeared
landscaped by European cash

and when I return to Wales
the same imported grass

mining cashed in for good

Season Of Goodwill (Jointly Written)

Pause for a moment
Lend an ear

No one told the miner
there was chicken to be had
so he stayed underground at Christmas
and the ironmaster was glad

Glad he was earning money
for times like the ferrous rock
were hard

But while there was someone else
to hammer and hack the seam
he could cook his goose in peace
in his yule-warm house
and his nails would remain clean

Meanwhile down below
the miner chipped
and his canary chirped
a featherweight carol
of Christmas cheer
of chicken and goose for the chewing

And that was the canary's undoing . . .

Geoff Jones
John Alcock
Christmas 2005

Sheep Farm

Far down the hill from the cruck house
a matchstick figure leans

hay bale slung across back
as if carrying a cross

the steep hillside stirs
and through wintered bracken

sheep slowly track
to their feeding station

inside his locked paddock
a redundant collie

tips up his empty bowl
and strains his neck

air barking in protest

My Home

My home is not my Welsh valley of today...

green rounded landscapes
clear sparkling rivers and exploring fish

My home was better

black slurried tumuli
rivers running red with industrial rust

cinder boulders abandoned trams and rails
vast natural playgrounds

My home is not my Welsh mountains of today
where red kites swoop off rock strewn roofs

distant Beacons shine
and Sugar Loaf sweetens the view

My home was better

cooling down in the sheep dip
and cold mountain stream

while steelwork smokestacks
shook out blankets of constant cloud

My home is not my Welsh village of today
estate agent signs like flags at half-mast

My home was better

gossiping streets jam packed buses
shop queues post war rationing
wives scrubbing front doorsteps
steelworkers on shifts and miners racked with coughs

My home was better . . .

Cenotaph

Tomorrow
the instruments will lie silent

Today we bang drums
blow trombones trumpet last posts
do our two-minute duty

Tomorrow
we will forget pomp and circumstance

Today we haul flags
dip standards in respect
stand silence still

Tomorrow
lapels without poppies

Today we remember the dead
dead hymns, dead prayers
left eyes we march memory past

Tomorrow
we will go bareheaded

Today black bowlers, berets red, green, white, black,
Paras, artillery, fusiliers, tank corps, convoys
and St Dunstan's blind to it all

Tomorrow
we will return to the future

Today we age back over time
exterminating war thoughts
as we dismember

Tomorrow
we will make barbed comments

Today barbed wire memories

Tomorrow we'll keep a low profile

Today we go over the top

War Cemetery

Hundreds of South Wales Borderers
surrounded our small group
but no conflict

we had already surrendered
to their silence
on entering the French cemetery

it hung heavily
smothering us
into our own silence

we shuffled uneasily together
uncomfortable at the sudden
consequence of war on home grown men

anxious to get it right
not wanting to offend
we huddled closer

heads bowed
as Bill Morris our chairman
asked us to join him

in *The Lord's My Shepherd*
I shall not want
He makes me to lie down
in green pastures

which I couldn't see
through a wall of tears
that drowned the
rest of the words

Brynmowr RFC Rugby Tour Easter 1962

Violin

It rests in ruffled satin of royal blue
opened after many years hidden away
as if your memory was concealed too
I am silent and don't know what to say

just admiring its beauty as I once did you
graceful slender of sparkling eye
not knowing what life would put you through
when you had no chance to say goodbye

to a life of joy and your treasured girls
not knowing this instrument was really you
where you lay your chin beneath black curls
and sawed and plucked as you used to do

and once again the music begins to play
as our daughter strums your yesterday

Black Dog

Churchill called it his black dog – I now know why –
for it crept up on me one day having sniffed my scent

it was not a pit bull or Rottweiler
that would savage in an instant

but one that circled like a hyena
biding his time then darting and biting

when I was off guard
until I was in terror of his presence

unable to see through the constant darkness
but I knew he was there

head on prostrate paws
ears flattened just waiting to pounce

growling authority
teeth exposed and flexing claws

that could rip me to the bone
and even though I sought help

he was not slow in bringing me to heel
until I wondered if I would ever escape

his clutches tied to that long lead
but one day I caught him off guard

and for all my pain and sorrow
I gave him a bloody good kicking

becoming his master once again

Memos

The day bursts into life
when I open my diary

the lists shouting
for attention

phone calls
shopping
library
lawns
bank
golf

words that do what I tell them
showing I'm the boss

of my nouns
now I'm retired

and in control
of my tenses

Made Up

Guerlain of Paris
compact case

circular to fit
the palm of one hand

while the fingers
of the other

apply its contents
eye shadow

blusher
lip gloss

changing looks
over the minutes

and years
until in the end

it's the undertaker
who gets to do the job

Too Young

They tried to tell us we're too young
in those far off fifties

now I'm way beyond my own fifties
I remember they tried to contain

the thrust of those teenage years
pent up and shackled by conformity

until the Rock 'n' Roll explosion blew away the control
never to be lived again

and parents envied a freedom
experienced in the Charleston and flapping years

before war and depression taught them
they were too young too

The Yellow Balloon
(with apologies to William Carlos Williams)

So much depended
on the grasp of that little boy

as the yellow
balloon

      rolled
    over and
      over

trapped

in the backwash
of the black weir

Kitchen

(i) The Kettle

That kettle always whistled its way to work
in spite of the hot road travelled

letting off steam
knowing it was advisable

rather than boiling over
in fury

(ii) To The Saucepan from The Kettle

You've got some sauce
coming along now and again
when all the work's been done

I give you all the help I can
then you go and pour it all away
as if it didn't matter

I can't get a handle on you at all
all I know is that without me
you'd dry up in no time

Smiles

Behind smiles
people live

forming fronts
as shopkeepers portray wares

people peering in
wondering what's behind them all

some genuine in appearance
honest open and welcoming

others disguising ambition and greed

and the enigmatic
concealing secrets in corners

back store rooms where no one can go

and the one shuttered and closed
hiding what might have been

behind smiles
where people live

The Challenge

It took some time
getting it together

struts of wood clashing
strangers to each other

others waiting
impatient frustrated

while I cursed the design
attempting different techniques

self conscious of the pity
and amused eyes

or even unwelcome sympathy
as I tried another approach

to swing the damned battens
slot notches becalm flapping canvas

sand shifting beneath my feet
before sinking gingerly at last

into the seat
of the ruffled deck chair

All In The Mind

In my mind I can sidestep an opponent
in reality the knee suffers from arthritis

I could run that marathon
if the back did not need an operation

I could cock the wrists on the upswing every day
if I could have cortisone injections

shoelaces and soft mattresses I can do without
and the stairs will soon be superfluous

when I was young I was told
that sport was good for me

and it's true for I'm still enjoying mind games
it's the body that can't keep up

Haiku

(i) Recall

Stooped umbrella man
sharpening bone-handled knives
stone wheel turns – his world

(ii) Quiet

Leaning on shovels
the whole workday before them
stilled council workers

(iii) Contentment

Escaped from noon sun
the dog dozes in shadows
sleeping his own dreams

The Wardrobe

When you turned the key
after I had gone
and opened the doors

on my past
to dust away the memories
of our many years

did you sit on the edge of the bed
you warmed for me in winter
and stare at the emptiness

I left you with
even though you thought our
family idyll would never end?

Or did you cry in your seclusion
remembering that autumn day
you waved your future goodbye

to an only son leaving home
as he caught the train
to a world elsewhere?

Where The Boots Take You

I shall put on the boots and walk backwards to home
where I will find a different pair

hard black leather and hobnails
hammered in by Dad to eke out his patience and pay

to walk up the side of the Milfraen
or Mynydd-carn-y-cefn's upper slopes

unspoiled by the spoils of coalmining
where we sat and chewed the juicy grass

our own cigarettes like the Woodbine packets
Dad sent me to buy in the Forties

and looked down on the adults
we looked up to during the hot days

when tarmac like black chewing gum
sought out our crêpe soled sandals

soon abandoned when we found
the new streamlined laced daps*

enabled us to run like the wind
wafting around our encased valley

before we resentfully replaced them
with summer's hibernating hobnails

daps – plimsolls

The Square Café

Sitting in the Italian café
at Formica tables

in Brynmawr Square
and sucking hot Vimto

through long lasting straws
we watched the large breasted Rita

steam heat the milk
throwing smiles and knowing glances

over her shoulder
as she grasped the lever

exhausting the hissing steam
like a train gathering speed

We were teenage passengers
riding long winter evenings

when time stood still
only moved by Elvis's

All Shook Up
from the corner juke box

revolving in lazy circles
but soon to break all records

both his and ours
in the rush to the demanding sixties

Uncle's Shed

He never kept it locked that brick built shed
adjoining the back garden footpath
trusting the community's respect

and curiosity to keep well away
from what it concealed
only open to my eyes

one day when I ventured secretly
into its silence and shadows
breathing the reek of engine oil

like a dog sniffing the air
trying to work out
from whence it came

workbench and wall tools
a vague backcloth
my eager eyes settling

on the motorbike and sidecar
standing silently together
hand in hand like lovers

nestling against each other
before venturing out
under village scrutiny

Climbing on the leather seat
I bent low across the handlebars
my worries of discovery disappearing

as I leaned against the camber of the TT circuit
throttle fully opened Norton screaming beneath me
battling for position with The Duke*

roaring up the final straight shoulder to shoulder
chequered flag drawing nearer ever nearer
my heart pumping furiously like the pistons below me

suddenly losing grip and sliding out of control
as I heard the sound of the latch
lifting behind me

*Geoff Duke: 1950s World Motor Cycling & Isle of Man TT
Champion*

I Know

As a boy
running down
the coal tip
chasing
the escaping
bouncing ball
I tripped
and sprawled
on waiting glass

crimson slashed
my small white palms

now when people remark on the
blue etched miner's scars
I'd like to lie and boast
of the plummeting cage
shovelling in low tunnels
manhandling black boulders
and the covering of dust
that coated my father
burrowing underground

but my computer-soft hands
give away the truth
he worked
and wanted for me

Recalling Snow

The branches of the pines bending
under the wind's anger refused to lie down
liberating superfluous needles on our patio

unlike the silver birches beyond
whose yellow leaves swirled and danced
like snowflakes

poles apart from those in Nantyglo
falling softly in the late evening
illuminated by a yellow street lamp

opposite my bedroom window
as I knelt and stared at the floating flakes
dreaming of tomorrow when the village would lie silent

drifting under dunes of white
Red and White buses imprisoned in depots
cars chained or pushed along snow avenues

by passers-by who leaned and panted
until the rear wheels
suddenly became live again

machine gunning snow
over trousers and slipping shoes
while housewives plotting precarious courses

on frozen pavements
laughed loudly in the still air
its temperatures sinking as the day wore on

hardening our sledge runs and drawing
 us away from the adult world
into our own and welcome darkness

Beneath The Bypass

Buried beneath the bypass
are the playgrounds of my past

of Ebbw Fach a rushing stone strewn stream
we dared each other

to leap across in dry mouthed flight
a wet boot length too far

splashed landings drawing howls
of delight from the bank behind

Near the water's edge
cinder boulders remnants of an iron age

squatted like mammoths and on their backs
we sat like kings ruling the valley

our miniature village above
and the black scarred Mynydd-carn-y-cefn behind

pensive silences shattered
by the squealing brakes of a panting train

pausing for breath at the GWR station
disgorging people through slamming doors

recollecting a semaphored guard
then snorting triumphantly on to Brynmawr

and the end of the line
now buried beneath the bypass

Brynmawr: town at the head of the valley

The World Was Not So Old Then

In the Fifties
the world was not so old then

but very grey

we lived under grey slates
looked out on mining tumuli

ate grey rationed bread
rode bikes along dusty tarmac

and spotted grey Standard cars

Mam even dressed me in fashionable grey
suit shirt and socks

before I rebelled in that late decade
for my world was not so old then

but very blue

we strolled under *Blue Skies*
kissed under a *Blue Moon*

climbed up *Blueberry Hill*
Sang our way

over the *Blue Ridge Mountains of Virginia*
and laced up *Blue Suede Shoes*

that danced us
through the Rock 'n' Roll years

now when I look back
through the closing windows

of the last century
the world was not so old then

nor so grey as it is now

Covered

(i) Home Guard Rifle

My father brought it
home

guard us I thought
laid it across the long oak table

large heavy
just like Dad

I reached up
touched the barrel

it frightened me
with its coldness

(ii) Identity Card '49

I found it in the desk drawer
unseen for many years
as if hiding its own identity

National Health Number
name and address
but no photograph

buff coloured creased care worn
oblivious
to the passing years

but still able
to prove
who I am

Welsh Wives

They stood about having
endless conversations
in shops or on pavements

no doubt opening with the weather
followed by ailments - theirs and yours
then reprocessing gossip heard earlier
or beginning a new cycle

shopping for family food
an all day village adventure
of tasting haggling complaining
and comparing prices

until they arrived home
tired but satisfied they had shopped
within the planned budget
and all within a few hundred yards

every Friday the same
every day carrying
the same task
washing ironing cooking cleaning

especially the front room
kept for best but never used
and Saturdays scrubbing the pavement
for the non-existent weekend

in service to husbands coming off shifts
while theirs never ended

Ossie Lovett

We loved you Ossie Lovett
we loved to shout and tease
we loved to see you riled
then did as we damned well pleased

loved to see you coming
battered trilby on one side
shouted insults fore and hind you
ran away in haste to hide

loved to hear you shuffling
body racked with cough
cheap jibes we threw at you
unheard as we ran off

loved to see your shoulders shaking
eyes rolling in your head
welcome additions to our playing
before we went to bed

loved your pavement spitting
as you tried to clear your lung
passers muttered angrily
at the chant of cheek we sung

we loved you Ossie Lovett
and now you're up above
I sometimes think and wonder
if you hated all that love

Classroom

(i) Ruler

You've always been straight with me
it's me who's slipped up
and made a mess of things

(ii) Fountain Pen

Always sucked up to me
but dropped ink bombs
when I wasn't attending

(iii) Pencil

Arrayed in a variety of colours
sometimes soft and pliable

sometimes hard
it's then I find you difficult to forget

for you always leave an impression

(iv) Compass

And I thought you were
going to help me find my way

instead of sending me
round in circles

(v) Protractor

You may be only a half circle
but you certainly give me

the angle
on everything

(vi) Pencil Box

I'll always remember my first day at school
I'll always remember you swivelled as a rule

revealing more pencils and fountain pen
but sadly I'll never use you again

for you've gone out of fashion I believe
or are you keeping something else up your sleeve?

(vii) Satchel

In the early years I kept you at arm's length
but as we grew up together

assisting me in my work
you became more than just a friend

I hugged you in my arms
treasured your company

but when you became
old and worn and clinging

I abandoned you
for someone young and trendy

(viii) Window

A face for all seasons

tear drops of rain
run down your cheeks

snowflakes
melt on your breath

wind rattles your bones

you always admit the sunshine

never hide anything

for you know

I always see through you

Dymock Church*

Sandstoned church edged
by April water meadows
river red with recent rains

lies silenced
by lost congregations
except in one small corner

where the Georgians' verse
almost forgotten
finds sanctuary

still protesting on
yellowing manuscripts
against Tennyson's 'dead poetry'

the fading black words
struggle for attention
some verses inked red

like the blood of Thomas**
given in another April country
long muddied in beliefs

Gloucester
*** Edward Thomas died Easter Monday 1917 Western Front
France*

Roston Chapel*

The faded black board
makes us all heartily welcome

*'No collection
and hymn books provided for everyone*

hundred and thirty five years later
I pass through the door

and tread the wooden
stairs to Norbury Lecture Room

the empty pews
of Primitive Methodism

no longer hear
the burning words from the lectern

never cluttered
by statue crosses stained glass windows

no pious priest stood
at the communion altar table

Behind the silent organ
a Holy Bible rests in dust

congregational ghosts
crowd in on me

I shut the door sealing tight
their fervent past

* Derbyshire

Panxworth Church*

Ordnance Survey Map
Church (disused)

Long body removed
no longer offering a service

just a flint-stoned tower remains
high above flat fields

fertile earth sending up
fingers of sinuous ivy

relentlessly reaching
for its bell windowed throat

ignoring the gargoyles' glares

In the graveyard below
past congregations lie

suffocated by brambles
and blankets of wild grass

unable to prevent the choking
of their neglected religion

Norfolk

Cathedral

Likened to Auden's
ocean going liner

it lies anchored and mothballed
reeking familiar age

for centuries its crew continually changing
captains shipped elsewhere or dying on the bridge

in service
to passengers some faithful others just along

for the trip
cruising through dangerous waters shirking duty

leaving it all
to The Master

Passing On

Full of eagerness and optimism
of wanting to walk my past

my eyes swept our main street
swept up by our road sweep

all those years ago

the street our football pitch
seemed narrower

touchlines marked out in yellow
ready to penalise offenders

it was the chapels that eroded
remnants of buoyancy

once pulpits of erupting fervour
now silent and extinct

my Hermon dead and buried
beneath a health centre

Bethlehem and Bethania
betrayed by bulldozers

Ebenezer Primitive Methodist
disfigured by hoardings

Bethel eyes black and shuttered
and losing face under

the wrath of Welsh weathers
all wrecked my recollections

at the bottom of an overgrown lane
I found Berea's gate half open

ready to admit more chapters
but the memories

had passed on

Eisteddfod

It gathers us in from our mountain valley or plain
a magnet attracting people

from both poles of Wales
people to be immersed in a culture

of music language song
always resurfacing

to sail the horizons of time

the harps will sing in the vales
the choirs reach out for the hills

and the wordsmiths beat out their verse
uniting us as a nation of welcome

for the festival renews us
renews our passions

renews our pride
renews our very soul

of Welshness

Returning

No sign of a ditch or dyke
as we swept down the incline above Wye

just a dragon of welcome on the border
crossing into Cymru and Sir Fynwy*

historically ambiguous as a Marcher boundary
now placed where it always belonged

always the same
quickening beat of emotions

regaining the passions of the Silures
people of the rocks

Gwent, Brycheiniog and Morgannwg
who threw back the legions of invaders

the further we push into the land
the more we feed off fields and trees

all overshadowed by Pen-y-Fal and Blorenge
settings changing in colour

by clouds fleeing above the landscape
as if painted by an artist

mixing our destination in familiar hues

* *Monmouthshire*